Sassy Sloth

THIS EDITION
Produced for DK by WonderLab Group LLC
Jennifer Emmett, Erica Green, Kate Hale, *Founders*

Editor Maya Myers; **Photography Editor** Nicole DiMella; **Managing Editor** Rachel Houghton;
Designers Project Design Company; **Researcher** Michelle Harris; **Copy Editor** Lori Merritt;
Indexer Connie Binder; **Proofreader** Susan K. Hom; **Series Reading Specialist** Dr. Jennifer Albro

First American Edition, 2025
Published in the United States by DK Publishing, a division of Penguin Random House LLC
1745 Broadway, 20th Floor, New York, NY 10019

Design copyright © Dorling Kindersley Limited 2025
Text and Illustration copyright © WonderLab Group LLC 2025
24 25 26 27 10 9 8 7 6 5 4 3 2 1
001–345519–April/2025

All rights reserved.
Without limiting the rights under the copyright reserved above, no part of this publication may be reproduced, stored in or introduced into a retrieval system, or transmitted, in any form, or by any means (electronic, mechanical, photocopying, recording, or otherwise), without the prior written permission of the copyright owner.
Published in Great Britain by Dorling Kindersley Limited

A catalog record for this book is available from the Library of Congress.
HC ISBN: 978-0-5939-6596-2
PB ISBN: 978-0-5939-6595-5

DK books are available at special discounts when purchased in bulk for sales promotions, premiums, fund-raising, or educational use. For details, contact:
DK Publishing Special Markets, 1745 Broadway, 20th Floor, New York, NY 10019
SpecialSales@dk.com

Printed and bound in China
Super Readers Lexile® levels 500L to 610L
Lexile® is the registered trademark of MetaMetrics, Inc. Copyright © 2024 MetaMetrics, Inc. All rights reserved.

The publisher would like to thank the following for their kind permission to reproduce their images:
a=above; c=center; b=below; l=left; r=right; t=top; b/g=background
Alamy Stock Photo: Blickwinkel / Lundqvist 15br, CarverMostardi 27, Feargus Cooney 18bl, Rosanne Tackaberry 28cl, 28cr, 29b; **Dreamstime.com:** Amilevin 24b, Anne Amphlett 21cr, Artrosestudio 6br, Bbgreg 24cla, Chernetskaya 13crb, Harry Collins 10br, Dmstudio 14bc, Erin Donalson 24-25 (Background), Kim Hammar 13bl, Janossygergely 8, Jenhuang99 3, Kjersti Joergensen 11, Kungverylucky 12, Ladadikart 6c, 24bc, Brian Magnier 17c, Tatiana Morozova 25b, Brooke Parish 28t, Alina Pavlovska 22br, Seadam 11tl, Sensvector 17bc, Wrangel 9, 30;
Getty Images: De Agostini Picture Library 20; **Getty Images / iStock:** E+ / KenCanning 16, E+ / Webguzs 24ca, Efenzi 7b, 25tr, Fendy Hermawan 15bc, Rini Kools 18-19, Mark Kostich 6-7, Evgeniya_Mokeeva 1bl, 5cr, 15crb, 25 (Props), 29crb, 30br, Passakorn_14 1c, Webguzs 4-5; **naturepl.com:** Photo Ark / Joel Sartore 25ca;
Shutterstock.com: Inspired By Maps 26b, Alfredo Maiquez 14b, Kristel Segeren 23

Cover images: *Front:* **Dreamstime.com:** Gomolach br; **Getty Images / iStock:** Enrico Pescantini;
Spine: **Getty Images / iStock:** Enrico Pescantini

www.dk.com

Sassy Sloth

Becky Baines

Contents

6	In the Slow Lane
10	In the Chill Zone
14	Sloth Superpowers
16	Super Moms
18	Prehistoric Powerhouses

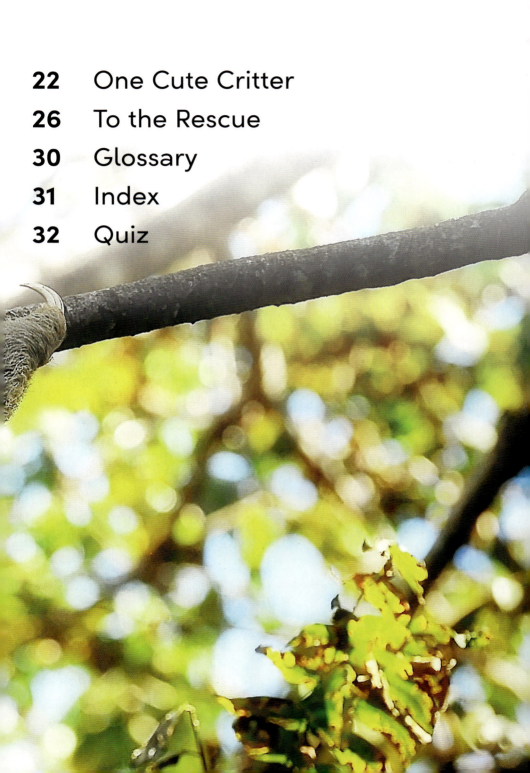

22	One Cute Critter
26	To the Rescue
30	Glossary
31	Index
32	Quiz

In the Slow Lane

What's that up in the tree? Is it leaves? A bird's nest? No. It's a sloth!

Sloths spend most of their lives hanging from branches. They live in the tippy tops of trees in the rainforests of Central and South America. When they move, they do so verrryyyyyy slooowwwwllllllyyyyy.

It can be hard to tell they're moving at all!

Three-Toed Sloths

- Four different species
- Weigh up to 10 pounds (4.5 kg)
- Three toes on all four limbs
- Only eat leaves of certain trees
- Look like they're wearing a black mask around their eyes
- Sometimes sit upright in the fork of a tree

Two-Toed Sloths

- Two different species
- Weigh up to 17 pounds (7.7 kg)
- Two toes on their front limbs and three on their back
- Bigger eyes and a lighter coat
- Eat various foods
- Light brown fur on their faces
- Hang upside down almost all the time

Yeah, and I'm the cuter one.

In the Chill Zone

These happy nappers sleep a lot! They can snooze anywhere from 8 to 20 hours a day. When they are awake, they inch across the rainforest treetops. They go in and out of the shade.

Zzzzz

From Fluffy to Toughy

Sloths in defense mode might surprise you. They look like tree-loving teddy bears. But they can hiss, shriek, claw, and bite their way out of danger.

I feel the need, the need for speed!

Sloths only climb up to eight feet (2.4 m) per minute. The slow movement helps hide them from predators. Big cats and hawks hardly know sloths are there.

Hungry sloths dig into a rainforest specialty—leaves! They hook their curved claws around a branch. They pull it into their mouths. Sloths don't have sharp front teeth. They smack their lips together to break down their food.

Two-toed sloths sometimes sneak a bite of bugs, bird eggs, berries, and seedpods.

But a leafy-green diet doesn't offer much nutrition. Nutrition is fuel for bodies. That's why sloths move so slowly!

All that chewing sure makes me sleepy!

The Scoop on Poop

Sloths spend most of their lives up in the treetops. They are safe from predators there. They only travel down to the forest floor once a week. Why? To go poop! Once a week is enough! Their digestive systems are very slow.

Sloth Superpowers

Climbing

Sloths have three- to four-inch claws. They also have a very strong grip. This makes them rock-star tree climbers. They can hold 100 percent of their body weight with one hand! If they do fall, sloths can tumble over 100 feet to the ground and just shake it off.

Olympic trials, here I come!

Swimming

Crawling on land, sloths can only move about one foot (30 cm) per minute. But in water, they can travel up to 44 feet (13.4 m) a minute! They float easily. Their long arms also make perfect paddles. The rainforest is, well, rainy. Rivers form when it rains a lot. Sloths drop out of the trees and travel by river. The water helps protect them from pesky predators.

Super Moms

The mother of the year award goes to...sloths! These mighty mamas climb down to lower branches to give birth. That way, there's less of a chance their babies will be hurt if they fall. And they do it while hanging...upside down!

A sloth baby is born weighing as much as a grapefruit. It has teeth and sharp claws ready to go! It clings to its mom's chest for the next six months. It drinks the mom's milk. It also starts eating leaves from her mouth after just a week!

Call Your Mother

After six months, it's time for the baby to let go of mom for good. But they will keep in touch! Sloth moms and their pups share their territory. The pairs stay in contact through loud calls.

Ring!

Ring!

Prehistoric Powerhouses

Ground sloths were a group of giant sloths. They went extinct about 11,000 years ago. The smallest species was the size of a black bear. The biggest was larger than an elephant! Unlike today's sloths, these giants lived on the ground.

South American giant sloth skeleton in the Natural History Museum in London

Some even lived *under*ground. Scientists have discovered huge tunnels in South America. They go hundreds of feet into the earth. These burrows of ancient ground sloths are lined with claw marks.

What's weirder than a giant sloth digging up your yard? One in your swimming pool, maybe! Paleontologists have dug up clues that some ground sloths lived in the water. They dined on plants from the seafloor.

Megatherium

Dinosaurs had *T. rex* Sharks had *Megalodon*. Meet *Megatherium*!

This supersized sloth was taller than a two-story house. It roamed the world alongside humans for a few thousand years.

Do you like guacamole? *Megatherium* did you a favor! It was a veggie eater like sloths today. It ate tons of greens, berries, and fruits, including avocados. It swallowed the fruit whole. The seeds came out in its poop. New trees popped up wherever it went. Avocado trees all over the world would not exist without *Megatherium*!

Holy guacamole!

One Cute Critter

Look at that face! What makes these animals so darn cute? Science!

People find things with big heads and round faces adorable. This makes us want to take care of them. Scientists say certain things make a critter cute. Sloths have got them all!

☑ Big head
☑ Button eyes
☑ Round face
☑ Wide smile
☑ Soft and fuzzy
☑ Round body

Scientifically extreme cuteness? No wonder these fellas are superstars!

To the Rescue

Sloths need our help. They have become popular pets in some parts of the world. This makes them an easy target for animal traffickers. They look cuddly, but sloths are wild animals. They often don't survive capture.

Sloths are also being run out of their territory by humans. Humans cut down rainforest trees for buildings and farming. This makes it harder for sloths to find food. They are forced out of their homes.

But there is hope! There are a lot of people around the globe working to save sloths from traffickers and development.

How Can I Help?

Learn everything you can about sloths. Tell your friends! You can also raise money in your community. Donate it to sloth causes you care about.

People raise money to fight against animal trafficking. They create sloth bridges. These are ropes that hang above the highway so sloths can cross safely. They plant trees to make food sources easier for sloths to find.

Rescue organizations take in sloths that have been hurt. They raise baby sloths. They care for them to make sure the species can thrive. They want sloths to be around for a long, long time.

Glossary

Animal trafficker
A person who illegally steals, sells, or buys animals

Development
The process of changing a natural place into one occupied by people

Digestive system
The network of organs that helps your body absorb nutrients

Extinct
No longer living

Nutrition
Fuel to help your body grow

Paleontologist
A scientist who studies fossils

Territory
An area where an animal lives

Index

ancient ground sloths
18–21

animal traffickers
26–27, 28

avocados 21

babies 16–17, 29

claws 11, 12, 14, 17, 19

climbing 11, 14, 16

cuteness 22–25

defense mode 11

food 12–13, 17, 19,
21, 28

ground sloths 18–21

hanging upside down
9, 16

helping sloths 26–29

leaves 12–13, 17

Megatherium 20–21

mothers 16–17

nutrition 13

pets 26

poop 13, 21

predators 11, 13, 15

prehistoric sloths
18–21

rescue organizations
29

sleep 10

sloth bridges 28

slow movement 7, 11,
13, 15

superpowers 14–15

swimming 15, 19

territory 27

three-toed sloths 8

two-toed sloths 9

underground sloths
19

Quiz

Answer the questions to see what you have learned. Check your answers in the key below.

1. What was Megatherium's favorite food?
2. How often do sloths climb to the ground?
3. True or false: Sloths are excellent swimmers.
4. How do sloth moms have their babies?
5. What is a sloth's favorite food?

1. Avocados 2. Once a week 3. True 4. They hang upside down
5. Leaves